Time to Celebrate!

LET'S GO TO A COOKOUT!

By Benjamin Proudfit

Please visit our website, www.garethstevens.com. For a free color catalog of all our high-quality books, call toll free 1-800-542-2595 or fax 1-877-542-2596.

Library of Congress Cataloging-in-Publication Data

Names: Proudfit, Benjamin, author.
Title: Let's go to a cookout! / Benjamin Proudfit.
Description: New York : Gareth Stevens Publishing, 2020. | Series: Time to celebrate! | Includes index.
Identifiers: LCCN 2018044077| ISBN 9781538238905 (pbk.) | ISBN 9781538238929 (library bound) | ISBN 9781538238912 (6 pack)
Subjects: LCSH: Cookouts–Juvenile literature. | Outdoor cooking–Juvenile literature.
Classification: LCC GT2955 .P76 2020 | DDC 641.5/78–dc23
LC record available at https://lccn.loc.gov/2018044077

First Edition

Published in 2020 by
Gareth Stevens Publishing
111 East 14th Street, Suite 349
New York, NY 10003

Editor: Kristen Nelson
Designer: Katelyn E. Reynolds

Photo credits: Cover, p. 1 Topic Images Inc./Getty Images; pp. 5, 9, 13, 15, 17, 23, 24 (grill) Rawpixel.com/Shutterstock.com; p. 7 Halfpoint/Shutterstock.com; p. 11 Wiktory/Shutterstock.com; pp. 19, 24 (campfire) Dmitry Sheremeta/Shutterstock.com; pp. 21, 24 (fireflies) Suzanne Tucker/Shutterstock.com.

Printed in the United States of America

CPSIA compliance information: Batch #CS19GS: For further information contact Gareth Stevens, New York, New York at 1-800-542-2595.

Contents

Cookouts are fun.
We will eat and
play outside!

Our family comes over.
They brought food!

Sally brought fruit.

Aunt Jackie made potato salad.

Uncle Peter
uses the grill.
He makes
us hamburgers.

Dan and I swim while we wait.

Dinner is ready!
We eat together
at the table.

It is getting dark.
Dad starts a campfire.

We see fireflies!

What a great time!

Words to Know

campfire

fireflies

grill

Index